Ready for RUSH

Ready for RUSH

The Must-Have Manual for Sorority Rushees!

Sister-to-Sister Advice from
BONNIE & DEBBIE THORNTON

Hamblett House Inc.

Copyright © 1999 Bonnie and Debbie Thornton.
All rights reserved.
No part of this book shall be reproduced, stored in a retrieval system, or transmitted by any means, electronic, mechanical, photocopying, recording, or otherwise, without written permission from the publisher.

No patent liability is assumed with respect to the use of the information herein. Although every precaution has been taken in the preparation of this book, the publisher and authors assume no responsibility for errors or omissions. Neither is liability assumed for damages resulting from the use of information contained herein.

Published by Hamblett House Inc., 4117 Hillsboro Road, Suite 103322, Nashville, TN 37215, hamblett@aol.com

Edited by Amy Lyles Wilson
Illustrations by Chuck McIntosh
Printed by Vaughan Printing
Book design by Gore Studio Inc.

Library of Congress Catalog Card Number
98-83138

ISBN: 0-9661049-2-7

99 98 — 3 2 1

To our parents,
*Leon and Barbara Thornton,
the two people who gave us life,
taught us about living, and continue
to encourage and strengthen us
every step of the way.*

Contents

	Introduction	ix
1.	In the Beginning	1
2.	Is Greek Life for You?	15
3.	Start Young	31
4.	Do Your Homework	45
5.	Stop, Look, and Sniff	59
6.	Is That What You're Wearing?	73
7.	Etiquette Essentials	87
8.	First Things First	99
9.	Showtime!	113
10.	Let the Good Times Roll	137
	Appendix	153

Introduction

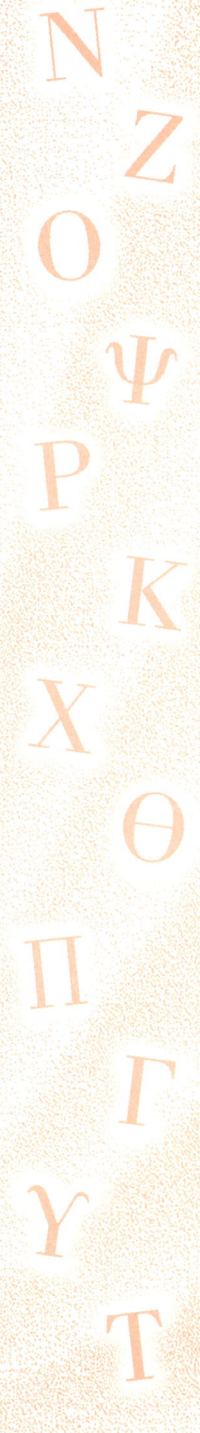

When graduation night arrives and you move your tassel to the right and toss your cap twenty feet in the air, you're not only a high-school graduate, you're also on the brink of adulthood.

Welcome to college life: new beginnings, new friends, new opportunities, and a new, independent you. Welcome to the threshold of a whole new universe—being on your own for the first time.

Adjusting to college life can be difficult. But being away from Mom's homecooked meals and Dad's wallet is the easy part. You've entered a world where no one even knows your name. You're going to have to start all over again, laying the groundwork for all sorts of opportunities, all the while making new friends. You can't rest on your parents' laurels, or your older sister's popularity. Now it's up to you.

During a Rush skit, the Kappa Alpha Thetas at the University of Kentucky sing, "Wouldn't you like to find a place where everyone knows your name?" You might recognize the lyrics, taken from the theme song of the television show *Cheers*. In order to ease your adjustment to college life and expand your social and academic horizons, we'd like to help you find a place where everybody knows your name. Not at the local pub, mind you, but in a sorority where

you are valued, respected, challenged, comforted, and admired.

The idea for this book came about when our niece Lacy, who is now a high-school senior, voiced her uncertainties about college life. She asked all sorts of questions about joining a sorority, as did her friends. They didn't know what to expect and felt completely overwhelmed. After answering countless questions, we realized that Lacy and her friends, along with many other young, college-bound women across the United States, were in the dark about Rush.

The two of us remember Rush week as being mentally, emotionally, and physically demanding, yet those seven days were some of the most important ones of our college years, for we each found a home away from home. Greek life was so meaningful for us that we wanted to share it with others. This is our gift to Lacy and all the other rushees out there. We can't guarantee that our advice will get you into the sorority of your choice, and some of you will decide that sorority life is not for you. But we do promise you'll be prepared and armed with an idea of what to expect. Surely such insight will help make your Rush week an enjoyable and fulfilling experience. Sorority life isn't for everyone, but if you're inclined to check it out, take a peek inside these pages for a sneak preview. Now get ready, get set, Rush!

Bonnie and Debbie Thornton

Ready for RUSH

CHAPTER 1

In the Beginning

The first known women's fraternity (later referred to as a *sorority*) was founded in 1851. More than three million women have experienced Greek life since then. Alpha Delta Pi was founded under the name of the Adelphean Society at Wesleyan Female College in Macon, Georgia. Pi Beta Phi followed soon thereafter at Monmouth College on April 28, 1867. The first society to use Greek letters was the Kappa Alpha Theta sorority in 1870 at Indiana Asbury University (now DePauw University). These organizations and several others similar in purpose were organized and came to be known as sororities. As time

THE GREEK ALPHABET

Α	α	Alpha
Β	β	Beta
Γ	γ	Gamma
Δ	δ	Delta
Ε	ϵ	Epsilon
Ζ	ζ	Zeta
Η	η	Eta
Θ	θ	Theta

Ι	ι	Iota
Κ	κ	Kappa
Λ	λ	Lambda
Μ	μ	Mu
Ν	ν	Nu
Ξ	ξ	Xi
Ο	ο	Omicron
Π	π	Pi

Ρ	ρ	Rho
Σ	σ	Sigma
Τ	τ	Tau
Υ	υ	Upsilon
Φ	φ	Phi
Χ	χ	Chi
Ψ	ψ	Psi
Ω	ω	Omega

went on, these special clubs based on female bonding became more popular and proved to be the women's home away from home. They encouraged cultural growth, scholastic merit, virtuous living, community involvement, and overall leadership. The sorority epitomized the blossoming young lady. Almost a century and a half later, the sorority has become a cornerstone for college life. Idealism and friendship are promoted as the key elements of the groups today.

Each sorority's name is taken from two or three letters of the Greek alphabet. The names commonly contain a motto or belief that is known only by the members. While these letters don't mean anything to outsiders, they have deep symbolic value to the members. Each sorority has its own rituals, handshake, motto, flower, and symbol.

Each sorority is part of a national organization that reaches across the country. Campuses have branches of the sororities, called *chapters*. Each chapter is responsible for its day-to-day activities, but the sorority is governed by guidelines set by the national organization. These guidelines include acceptable behavior, dues, and established grade point average. All of these criteria must be met to remain a member in good standing. The

Four Phi Mu Friends Graduate, University of Mississippi, 1944

national organization is made up of alumnae who care deeply for their sorority and its reputation.

In order to provide good interrelations among sororities, the National Panhellenic Conference (NPC) was established in 1902. The NPC is responsible for recommending social standards and Rush guidelines. Twenty-six sororities are members of the NPC, whose function is not to govern but to advise. (A list of these sororities can be found at the end of this book.)

The National Pan Hellenic Council was organized in 1930 to oversee the primarily African American Greek organizations. These organizations' main emphasis is to provide service to the African American community as well as to their larger communities.

Laying the Groundwork for Success

Involvement in a sorority can be a terrific contribution to your college years. The process of joining a sorority begins with membership recruitment during *Rush*. Rush can best be described as a weeklong whirlwind of parties, in which you will meet hundreds of Greek women. Rush gives you a chance to get acquainted with all the sororities and to develop your own viewpoint as to where you fit best. You'll want to present yourself in your best light, and you are going to be confronted with tough decisions. Friends and family members may try to influence you, but this is your first time on your own, and it's time to begin making decisions for yourself. Many young women come into Rush with their minds already made up. Maybe they plan to *pledge* (accept an offer to join a certain sorority) where their sister is a member or where their mother is an alumna. Take your time and give each *house* (another word for sorority) a fair chance. Our belief is that we could have been happy at a number of different houses, and the three *preference* or *pref* night houses (last night of Rush, when you are invited back to a limited number of houses) would have been good choices for either of us. We encourage you to keep an open mind. You just might be surprised!

"Fraternity" and "sorority" are used often interchangeably when talking about women's Greek-letter societies. "Fraternity" comes from the Greek word "phrater," which means brother, sister, or clan. "Sorority" is based on the Latin word "soror," which means sister. Although many were founded and incorporated as women's fraternities before the word "sorority" was coined, the term "sorority" is used to distinguish women's groups from men's groups.

SISTER TALK

I knew before I went to high school that I wanted to join a college sorority, but I did not make up my mind which club to join until the last night of Rush. I liked two groups, but I felt more at home in the Kappa Delta (KD) house. After the decision was made, I never looked back.

Pledging a sorority at the small liberal arts college I attended provided me a ticket to be involved. From day one, opportunities abounded for me to take part in, do my part for, and feel a part of. Playing intramural sports, serving on the social committee, and being an officer gave an added dimension to my classroom education I might have ignored had I not joined the sorority.

I remember my first intramural flag football game. Every time I came near the ball, my sisters on the sidelines would cheer my name. I didn't even know they knew my name, but they did. I was not the football star, but I sure felt like it on that field. I had joined a team whose spirit had been forming for more than 50 years. It was easy for me to feel like an integral part of this group very quickly.

I was able to help others feel like they belonged when I served on the sorority social committee. I loved meeting new people, so I took pride in creating party themes and ways to help the guests mingle. It helped my friends—and me—expand our social circles.

By the time I was a senior in college, I was elected president of Kappa Delta. Not only was I engrossed with members of my own club, but as its leader, I also worked with the other sorority and fraternity leaders on campus issues, communicated with alumnae on plans, and associated with the national officers of Kappa Delta. Through my position as president, I improved my communication, organizational, and leadership skills. I felt I was giving back to a group that had given me a home for four years.

I would be remiss if I did not mention the friendships I made through KD. Not all the girls in my sorority were my best friends, but that common bond gave each of us a connection to each other—be it a running buddy, a study partner, or someone to fix up on a blind date. Today that connection still provides opportunities through alumnae. No matter what I'm involved with now, be it a parent's group at my children's school or a Junior League community project, there's always another KD who's doing it too.

Lauri Collins
B.A., M. Ed., development officer, wife, and mother of three

CHAPTER 1 CHECKLIST

- ☑ *Research sorority history.*
- ☑ *Get input from family and friends, but stay true to yourself.*
- ☑ *Find out if any women you admire were in a sorority.*
- ☑ *Keep an open mind!*

NOTES

CHAPTER 2

Is Greek Life for You?

Greek life will provide you with a great number of social, philanthropic, and athletic events in which to involve yourself. You'll also be required to attend the meetings, participate in activities, and commit to the principles and values upon which the sorority was founded. Your commitment of time and energy to your new sorority will determine the benefits you receive.

The Greek system varies from campus to campus, but Greeks usually sponsor dozens of campus activities. Sometimes the smaller campuses have the more active Greek communities.

Is Greek life for you? Think long and

hard about your answer. Are you a person who enjoys the company of like-minded people? Do you like having people readily available for studying or hanging out? Would you appreciate homecooked meals eaten with your friends? Do you participate in sports? Are you a team player? Are you interested in helping others by reaching out? Do you want to feel you have a home away from home? Are you prepared to meet certain financial obligations? If you answered yes to some or all of these questions, then it's likely that you are well-suited for Greek life. If so, pledging is the first step toward reaching that goal.

We realize that sorority life is not for everyone. It is an individual choice that must be considered thoughtfully and with great care. You may go through Rush and decide not to pledge. You may go through Rush and not get an invitation to join the sorority you hoped for. Many young women pride themselves on being *independents*, those not affiliated with the Greek world, and could not imagine participating in a system that functions on ceremony, tradition, and group activities. Thankfully, at college and university campuses across the country, there is room

PANHELLENIC CREED

"We, as undergraduate members of women's fraternities, stand for good scholarship, for guarding of good health, for maintenance of fine standards, and for serving, to the best of our ability, our college community. Cooperation for furthering fraternity life, in harmony with its best possibilities, is the ideal that shall guide our fraternity activities.

We, as fraternity women, stand for service through the development of character inspired by the close contact and deep friendship of individual fraternity and panhellenic life. The opportunity for wide and wise human service through mutual respect and helpfulness is the tenet by which we strive to live."

NATIONAL PANHELLENIC CONFERENCE

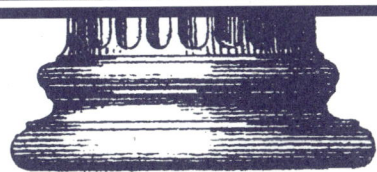

enough for each of you to follow your own heart.

It's All Greek to Me

It may seem overwhelming to you now, but there is no reason to panic. You don't have to learn the Greek language to join a sorority, but there are a few key terms that will help familiarize you with the process.

Active: A sorority woman who has completed the membership education and has been formally initiated.

Alumna: A sorority member who has graduated from college. The alumna is able to provide recommendations for girls wanting to pledge. Alumnae (plural of alumna) talents are utilized through guiding and advising the chapter.

Bid: A formal invitation to membership offered from a sorority to a rushee.

Big sister: An active assigned to a pledge to help her with any problems or adjustments that she may have.

Chapter: The local group of a larger, national social organization.

Fraternity: This is a homogeneous term that refers to both male and female Greek organizations, although many of us associate the term with a male group. Greek letters, rituals, and symbolic pins characterize the organizations.

Greek: A person who is called "Greek" is an individual who is a member of a fraternity or sorority.

Hazing: The immoral and illegal harassment of pledges. Usually involves degrading pranks and inappropriate treatment. If you hear of this happening, report it to someone in authority immediately.

House: This is used interchangeably with sorority (i.e., "Which 'house' are you a member of?")

Independent: A college student who is not a member of a sorority or fraternity.

Initiation: Process during which a pledge becomes an active. Usually involves a ritualistic ceremony designed to highlight the special aspects of the particular sorority.

Legacy: A prospective member whose grandmother, mother, or sister is an alumna or is currently an active in the sorority.

THE SURVEY SAYS...

In a recent, informal survey of sorority girls across the United States, we found that...

57% of the actives, ranging from second semester freshman to seniors, stressed that being prepared with interesting questions would make Rush parties more enjoyable and help avoid monotony.

39% of the actives polled felt the most important advice they could give is to be yourself. If you try to be something you're not, you will wind up in a house that you are uncomfortable with down the road.

33% of the Greek women polled urged rushees to get plenty of sleep. Rush is the biggest slumber party you have ever attended. You must discipline yourself to eat well and get plenty of rest.

30% of the sisters agreed that the biggest Rush fallacy is that all sorority girls are "Daddy's little rich girls." Contrary to rumor, there are no family financial checks made on rushees.

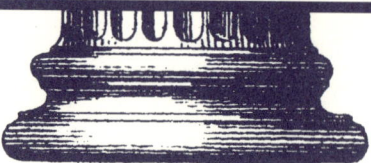

Little sister: A pledge who is assigned to an active or her "big sister." This relationship starts during the pledging period and continues throughout your years as a sorority member.

NPC: National Panhellenic Conference. This national governing body of sororities is made up of twenty-six member groups.

NPHC: National Pan Hellenic Council. This national governing body is made up of historically African American sororities and fraternities.

Pin: The pledge pin is an insignia used to designate a pledge of a particular sorority. An active pin is an insignia that designates an active member of a particular sorority.

Quota: The number of rushees that a chapter may pledge during Rush.

Recommendation: Also known as a "rec." A letter or phone call from an alumna introducing and suggesting consideration for a rushee to a particular sorority.

Rho Chi: Your Rush counselor.

Rush: A period when young women have the opportunity to meet actives in all houses through a round of

informal and formal parties. The rushee is given the chance to learn more about the various chapters and their members.

Silence: The period of time during Formal Rush when there is no communication between rushees and sorority members.

Sorority: A group of women who have been through formal initiation and are bound together by ritual ties, moral fiber, and common goals. This bond lasts a lifetime.

Suicide: Choosing to list only one sorority when you submit your list of sororities you wish to join at the end of Rush week. "Going suicide" is not recommended; chances are, you'll end up without a bid at all if you choose this limiting option.

Getting Along

As with any extended family, whether it is biological or social, not everyone sees eye to eye on everything. We urge you to keep in mind that with pledging there will be compromises. Yet, the rewards are great when you pledge with the sorority that best suits you.

If sports are your bag, after you pledge you can get involved with intramural activities. Tennis, powderpuff football, softball, soccer, golf, bowling, and just about any sport that strikes your fancy can probably be played on a team that represents your house. It's not only a great way to get to know your new sisters, but also to become active in the Greek community as a whole. You'll have a lot of fun and you'll get plenty of exercise. Personal experience reminds us that the first year of college can be good for an extra fifteen pounds, so stay active in order to work off any additional calories that might come your way. You're going to be staying up later, having more midnight pizza—all in all, having more fun. But there's always a price for such indulgences, and getting involved in intramural sports can be your way to pay the piper!

Pledging a sorority will provide you with an opportunity to develop your leadership skills and also an opportunity to get involved with the community at large. It you've chosen a school with a large campus, then you are probably living in a relatively large community, with lots of extracurricular activities just waiting for your special touch. Campaigning for a state senator, collecting money for a charity, volunteering for a nonprofit organization, working for a hospital, or helping fix up a nursing home are all activities that will enable you to grow as an individual through service to others.

Pledging a house will also open doors for you to meet influential and accomplished alumnae who take an active role with the chapter. If you need a part-time job, an alumna is the person to ask. There's a good chance that one of the alumnae will be able to point you in the right direction. If you're having a problem or you just need someone to listen to you, you'll have an experienced person to contact. The local alumnae will also be able to help you find a new church or other appropriate resources in the community.

The advantages of sorority life are not only immediate but can also reach far into your future. Who knows? You might meet your future husband on a blind date arranged by your big sister. And don't forget that being a member of a well-regarded sorority will look great on your resumé, and serve as an asset for you in simple terms of poise and etiquette. Yet, the greatest gift you'll receive from pledging is the lasting friendships you'll cultivate, for you are not just a Tri Delt or a Kappa for your college years alone. Instead, you are a sister for life.

SISTER TALK

Sorority membership seemed to be a natural choice for me, but the hoopla of formal Rush was not for me. So I waited until after Rush to accept invitations to visit several houses on campus. I also felt this "Informal Rush" gave me more control in the sorority selection process. It didn't take me long to select Delta Zeta. After going to my first dinner at the Delta Zeta house I knew this was the sorority for me. I felt part of a group, but not a part of a mold.

Looking back, I realize how sorority membership affected so many things in my life. As a sorority member living in a group home, you learn to share, organize, and prioritize. I am a better leader, a better public speaker, and more confident as an individual because of the events and activities sorority membership provided. I learned the value of volunteerism, philanthropic fundraising, and business management. More than anything

though, I learned about friendship. Still many years later, some of my most meaningful and long-lasting college friendships are with my sorority sisters. We continue to share the events and milestones in our lives.

After college, sorority continued to play a part in my life. As a new resident in a big city, I had few friends. So, I decided to attend a local alumnae meeting, and before long I had made several friends and was participating in many activities. Over time my participation would include committee chairmanships and executive offices.

As I get older the demands on my time are greater so I'm not always able to get involved in new sorority projects. However, I always find time to call a Delta Zeta sister, or write a quick note. No matter what I'm doing or where I'm living, my sorority friendships have remained strong. I guess, in the end, friends are still the best reason for joining a sorority.

Rachel Platt
B.A., human resources manager

CHAPTER 2 CHECKLIST

- ☑ Decide whether Greek life is really for you. Don't let peer pressure overwhelm your thinking.

- ☑ Familiarize yourself with some of the commonly used Rush and sorority terms.

- ☑ Become familiar with the Greek alphabet and pronunciations.

- ☑ Find out which sororities represent your particular interests. Maybe you're a track star and sorority XYZ sponsors lots of athletic competitions.

NOTES

NOTES

CHAPTER 3

Start Young

When does Rush begin? You might not know it, but Rush begins during your freshman year in high school! Your grades, activities, and interests combine to make you the rushee of the future. Well-rounded, involved young women excite the actives waiting for you on the front steps of the sorority houses. They are eagerly looking for pledges who will help their sorority be the best on campus. The actives are searching the entire group of rushees, numbering in the hundreds and thousands, for the overachieving, active, confident, and personable young women.

Grades, Grades, Grades!

We know you're tired of hearing this from your parents and your teachers, but trust us, they're right. We cannot overemphasize the importance of good grades. Most houses require a 2.5 to 3.0 grade point average for entering pledges. Sororities compete amongst themselves, and every semester they have a house grade point average that pits them against the other houses on campus. The Greek system has an impressive record of high academic achievement. Based on scholastic records, the all-sorority grade point average has not only been higher than the all-female grade point average for the same period of time, but higher than the all-university grade point average as well.

Such clubs as Future Business Leaders of America, Future Farmers of America, Future Homemakers of America, and Fellowship of Christian Athletes are all terrific clubs offered by most high schools. Get involved in one or more of these. Run for office, learn leadership, and develop your organizational skills. All these qualities will not only enhance you as an individual but will also make your resumé look terrific when you're going through Rush.

RUSH CALENDAR

SIX TO TWELVE MONTHS BEFORE RUSH BEGINS:

- List your honors, achievements, and activities. If your fact sheet or resumé is not impressive, get involved now!

- Make a list of your family's sorority affiliations.

- Talk with students at the college or university you will be attending in order to get a feel for the environment and the people.

- Talk with friends who are in sororities and let them know you are interested in Greek life.

- Start saving money for your Rush wardrobe.

- Get in shape. Establish an exercise program so you will look and feel your best when it comes time to leave for school.

THREE MONTHS BEFORE RUSH BEGINS:

- Make sure all of your relatives and family friends know you are planning to go through Rush.

- Have a flattering photograph of yourself made.

- Read a good etiquette book to brush up on your manners.

- Order personal tea cards.
- Prepare your personal resumé to distribute to those who will write recommendations for you.
- If possible, visit the campus where you will be attending and find out where the sorority houses are, so that you can get your bearings ahead of time.

ONE MONTH BEFORE RUSH BEGINS:

- Go on your Rush shopping spree.
- Start reading the newspaper every day, if you don't already.
- See a few current movies, which can serve as great conversation topics.
- Shedule an appointment at a beauty salon for two weeks before Rush begins.
- Confirm your dormitory assignment. You don't want any surprises here!

TWO WEEKS BEFORE RUSH BEGINS:

- Have a dress rehearsal to try on all of your outfits for each round of parties. Make sure everything is altered appropriately and that you have the right lingerie and accessories for each ensemble.
- Go on a last minute shopping spree for things you need.
- Have your hair cut and highlighted if

necessary.
- Practice applying cosmetics in natural light.
- Start packing for college!

TWO DAYS BEFORE RUSH BEGINS:
- Get a manicure.
- Iron or steam your wardrobe.
- Sleep late!
- Get together with your high school friends for a farewell luncheon.
- Finish packing for college.

THE DAY RUSH BEGINS:
- Get up early enough to have a nice relaxing breakfast.
- Try to stay calm. Meditate, exercise, listen to your favorite music, whatever.
- Begin dressing at least an hour before your have to meet your Rush group.
- Apply your makeup carefully and sparingly.
- Relax and be yourself. Remember, they are rushing you!
- Look in the mirror and smile!

Get involved in your church or temple by helping with a children's class. Join your parents when they're taking food to the elderly. Organize clothing and food drives for the less fortunate. Get on a committee and help raise money for Mothers Against Drunk Driving or another worthwhile cause you believe in. There are a host of opportunities just waiting for your input. You'll build your resumé *and* your character. Sorority actives aren't looking for girls who sat on the sidelines during their high school years. Instead, they hope to welcome women into their sorority's fold who are aware of the world around them. They're looking for the go-getters, for the people who care about their community and are proactive in getting out there and making a difference.

Make the Call

Formal Rush may occur either in the early fall or the spring. If your campus conducts an early fall Rush, you should receive information during the summer. If you don't get anything in the mail about Rush, contact the school's panhellenic office. Some campuses require freshmen to wait a semester to participate in Rush and others welcome freshman and other participants the week before classes begin. Give the Rush registration form lots of thought before filling it out. Take extra pains with good penmanship and make sure you present yourself as honestly and positively as possible. In fact, it's a good idea to make a copy of the form for practice, or to draft your answers on another sheet of paper before attacking the "real thing."

Fill in all the blanks, and include all offices or titles held in your extracurricular activities if appropriate. Mention awards earned, championships captured, and achievements garnered. If you've been a member of many organizations, yet held no titles nor received any outstanding awards, go ahead and brag anyway, just be clever in doing it. Highlight even the most minor awards in creative ways. For some reason our sister Susie was considered an awesome golfer when she went through Rush. Every prospective house thought she was a scratch golfer, even though she couldn't break 100. Now how did they get such an idea? On Susie's Rush registration form, she had listed that she was the captain of her high school golf team. What she didn't mention was that she was the only one on the golf team. So naturally she elected herself captain, unanimously. But don't mistake Susie's enhancing of her Rush appeal as a lie. It was nothing more than creative marketing!

If your campus holds a Deferred Rush, usually offered in winter or early spring, you'll probably see publicity for this sometime after arriving on campus. Deferred Rush allows young women to orient themselves to the university first and the Greek system second. Informal or Open Rush gives you the chance to join a sorority when Formal Rush is not taking place. (Some schools are offering Rush a little later in the first semester, after a week or so of classes.)

What Will It Cost You?

As the saying goes, "nothing in life is free." Sorority life is no exception, as it does come with a price tag. Fees vary from house to house and campus to campus. The pledge semester is more expensive because of one-time fees, such as for initiation. After the semester of pledging, you will be responsible for active dues each semester. It is estimated that costs to join a sorority represent about 1.5% of a student's total college expenses. Here's an estimated sample of what you might expect to pay.

Rush Registration Fee: $20 to $50
Pledge Semester: $500 to $900
Active Semester: $300 to $600

These numbers represent an average of various charges from several universities across the country and are not meant to be an exact indicator of what your school will charge. Some sororities offer payment plans to accommodate tight budgets. Financial aid and scholarships are also available from many chapters.

SISTER TALK

As the mother of three teenagers, I see the excitement and the anxiety they experience as each one approaches his or her college years. As a former teacher, I know that kids relate well to hearing "grown-ups" talk about their own fears and concerns, so I try to assure—and amuse—my own offspring with reflections of my wonderful college days of yesteryear. I especially enjoy telling stories about my experiences as a

member of a sorority. Although many things have changed since I was a Tri Delt (Delta Delta Delta) in the 1970s, the friendships I made back then have stood the test of time. Being in a sorority enhanced my total college experience. When my youngest sister went through Rush some ten years after I did, I did everything I could to ensure that she had a good experience at the Tri Delt house. She told me that she did, but she felt more comfortable with the Chi Omegas, and that's where she ended up. (And our mother was a Phi Mu!) Now I can only hope that my daughter, a creative artist type, will find her spot as well when it's her turn.

Ann Holifield
B.A., M.Ed., office manager, wife,
and mother of three

CHAPTER 3 CHECKLIST

☑ *Keep up your grades! Most sororities require at least a 2.5 to pledge new sisters. Sororities seek enthusiastic, athletic, and motivated young women, so participate in as many extracurricular and charitable activities as you can while in high school.*

☑ *Be aware of financial obligations of Greek life. Payment plans and financial aid may be available.*

☑ *Consider joining a sorority only if you are willing to uphold the obligations of membership, such as attending meetings, participating in philanthropic, social, and athletic activities, and adhering to sorority standards of conduct.*

NOTES

....
....
....
....
....
....
....
....
....
....
....
....
....
....
....
....
....

NOTES

CHAPTER 4

Do Your Homework

Even if you've graduated from high school, your homework is just beginning—for Rush, that is. First and foremost, you'll need to get letters of introduction, commonly referred to as *recommendations* or *recs* from any active sorority members or alumnae you know. Generally, in order to pledge a house, recs are required. Now is the time to check with your mother's friends, your grandmother's bridge partners, women for whom you've babysat, and your sister's pals. Women of all ages can write recs. The only requirement is that they have been initiated into the sorority. Keep in mind that if you're attending the University of Alabama and your mother's friend attended Ole Miss, she can still write a recommendation for the sorority of which she was a member. Sororities are national organizations, and their ties reach much farther than the edge of campus. Get as many recs as you can, for all the sororities on campus. Even if you don't think you are interested in a house, get a recommendation for it anyway. You never know when you might change your mind and discover that the house at the bottom of your sister's list, or the one that wasn't right for your friend, is the perfect house for you.

Well before Rush begins is the time for the people who know you and your family to offer their two cents' worth about how wonderful you really are! As a rule of thumb, you do not come right out and ask an alumna to write you a recommendation. But what you can do is make sure she knows that you are going through sorority Rush. Either mention casually your plans or ask your mother or best friend to mention that you are interested in pledging and that you could use her help. Usually the alumna will be happy to write a recommendation on your behalf, and if she does not already know all about you,

DO
- Remember names
- Act interested
- Make eye contact when talking with others
- Give small compliments
- Discuss hobbies, movies, goals, books
- Be witty and funny
- Have breath mints
- Let them know you like them
- SMILE

DON'T
- Say, "Hmm, I don't have a clue who you are."
- Act snobbish
- Look around at others while talking with someone
- Talk about other sororities or rushees
- Bring up politics or money
- Tell off-colored jokes
- Smoke
- Chew gum
- Let them know you think they're idiots
- Frown

she will probably ask for some personal information and a nice photo. It is good form to supply each person writing a rec for you with this information, even if the woman has known you since you were a kid. There's no way she could be expected to be aware of every accomplishment you've had over the years, so help her out. Supply the person writing the rec with a list of achievements, such as a fact sheet or a resumé, so that she can speak highly of you. Include such vital information as grade point average, ACT/SAT scores, parents' full names, address, sorority legacies, academic awards, honors, and personal and group responsibilities. Supply this information to the alumna with enough lead time so that she can get it to her sorority about a month before Rush begins. Before you leave for school, write thank-you notes to the alumnae that wrote recommendations for you. This reinforces your interest in the sorority and your grasp of proper etiquette.

    The best recommendations are accompanied with flattering and memorable photos of the rushee. Be sure to put your name on the back of your photo in case it should get separated from your recommendation. Many rushees send their senior pictures, and

Miss Kentucky 1998 Talks About Rush

"Rush is indeed a 'rush'— the anticipation of things to come; the excitement of the activities; the stress of peer pressure, physical exhaustion, and choices to be made; and the fear of rejection. My advice to young women preparing for Rush is: Research the sororities at your chosen school before you go, and gather as many recommendations as you can for each sorority that you will consider joining. Also, remember that a sorority at one university may not be of the same caliber at another university.

Go with an open mind. Give every sorority a chance and be careful about eliminating each one during the Rush process. Remember, what you are seeing during Rush week may not be exactly what you get later, so look deeper!

Give serious consideration to each philanthropy. Believe in your sorority's programs. Make your own choice. Don't be swayed by others. I authored this statement for use on my application for Miss USA: 'I am who I am and I stand for what I believe.' Know yourself and feel comfortable with who you are. You can find other young women who share your interests and your goals.

After you've made your decision and your college years are done, stay true to your sisterhood. Your sorority connections will serve you well throughout the years ahead if you have chosen well. But for now, relax, have fun, and start taking those vitamins!"

Nancy L. Bradley, Miss Kentucky USA 1998

SAMPLE FACT SHEET / RESUMÉ

Sarah Brackin Chandler
232 Anywhere Street
Savannah, GA 42230

Parents: Mr. and Mrs. Matthew Chandler
High School: Franklin-Smith High School, Class of 1999
G.P.A.: 3.8 on a 4.0 scale
SAT score: 1250

ACADEMIC ACTIVITIES AND AWARDS
- Beta Club: Freshman, Sophomore, Junior, and Senior Years
- Beta Club Secretary, Junior Year
- Beta Club Vice-President, Senior Year
- Future Business Leaders of America: Junior and Senior Years; Outstanding Student Leadership Award, Senior Year
- Spanish Club: Sophomore, Junior, and Senior Years
- $5,000 J.R. Hooten Memorial Scholarship, Senior Year, for outstanding school spirit and dedication to business studies

EXTRACURRICULAR ACTIVITIES AND AWARDS
- Tennis Team: Freshman, Sophomore, Junior, and Senior Years; ranked #12 in Georgia High Schools, Senior Year
- Cheerleader: Freshman, Sophomore, Junior, and Senior Years; squad placed second in Georgia State Championships
- Member of First Presbyterian Church Youth Choir
- Involved with local Habitat for Humanity, participated in fundraising and volunteer recruitment.

SORORITY AFFILIATIONS
Mother, Kappa Delta, University of Alabama
Sister, Chi Omega, University of Georgia

this is acceptable. But a shot highlighting your style and personality might also be an option. Such an original photo will stand out in the midst of hundreds of standard senior pictures being viewed by the actives. The photograph you send is your calling card, so make sure it's appropriate. It will be posted so the actives can become familiar with your face and name. Many sororities put these photographs on a projector during their preparation week in order to get to know you even better. Speaking from the voice of experience, it's important that your picture looks like you, and that it's a good picture.

Your Birthright

A *legacy* is a rushee who has a sister or mother, or even a grandmother, who was a member of a sorority. For example, Barbara was a Alpha Omicron Pi (AOΠ) at Brown University, so when her daughter Marcy went through Rush at Purdue, she was a legacy to AOΠ. She also pledged AOΠ. When Barbara's middle daughter, Cindy, participated in Rush at Brown, she was a double AOΠ legacy, but she pledged Pi Beta Phi (Pi Phi). When the youngest daughter,

Robbie, goes through Rush next spring at Southern Methodist University, she will be a double AOΠ legacy and also a Pi Phi. Both of these sororities, as well as other competing sororities, will be on the outlook for Robbie because of her close family ties.

Out of respect, legacies are treated a bit differently as far as selection goes. If a legacy is invited back to preference night, she is usually assured a bid. A sorority will give strong consideration to each legacy, and will generally cut legacies early in the process if the house does not think the young woman would be happy there. This allows the rushee to set her sights on a different house and avoid investing her time and energy with a house that probably is not right for her. Legacies are not guaranteed bids.

If you are not a legacy, don't be discouraged. You can pledge any house by letting them see what a great person you are. Never fear, you will just have to work a little harder on getting those all-important recommendations to each sorority before Rush. You want them to know you are coming and to be on the lookout for you!

It is estimated that membership in a Greek organization represents about 1.5% of a student's total college expense.

SISTER TALK

The friendships I made during my years as a Kappa Kappa Gamma (Kappa) have become lifetime friendships. Having come from a small town to a university with 27,000 students, I was overwhelmed. Kappa gave me a group of friends that eased the

transition to college life. In addition, my sorority gave me an opportunity to build leadership skills by planning fundraisers and holding various offices. As I look back on my college experience, there is no doubt that the best part of my college years were spent at the Kappa house. I have lived in three cities in the eight years since I have left college, and each time the alumnae group responded quickly to get me involved and help me meet new friends. Joining a sorority is one of the best decisions that I have made. It is my firm belief that sororities provide young women with much needed support and growth opportunities in today's universities.

Lori Wood
B.B.A., M.B.A.

CHAPTER 4 CHECKLIST

- ☑ Try to have recs for each sorority on campus. Because a house you don't know much about might turn out to be your favorite, keep an open mind and make your own decisions.
- ☑ Make sure every sorority member you know, current or alum, realizes that you are going through Rush.
- ☑ Develop a fact sheet that includes all key details about you and your high school years and give it to all alumnae writing recs on your behalf. Include a flattering photograph.
- ☑ Write thank-you notes to all who wrote recs for you or otherwise helped you prepare for Rush. Do this before you leave for school.
- ☑ Legacies can usually count on being given a special look, although no one is guaranteed a bid. If you are not a legacy, don't panic! It's not a prerequisite for sorority membership.

NOTES

NOTES

CHAPTER 5

Stop, Look, and Sniff

Do your homework. Know what reputation precedes a house. Keep in mind that the reputation will vary from campus to campus. A reliable way to find out what sorority has which reputation is to talk to people you know who already go to school there, including fraternity guys on campus. Ask them for one-word descriptions of each house. During Rush, sororities put their best faces forward. Try to obtain clarity on the various houses' reputations before Rush begins. This may help eliminate some confusion and make your decision easier in finding the right house for you.

Although sororities vary from campus to campus, there is usually one of each of the following types at each school. The Greek system is like a micro-universe. There are all types of people thrown together and inevitably the like kind find each other. Now it's up to you to figure out which group you want to belong to. So stop, look, and sniff.

Wealthy Wanda

This house is easy to spot. One house on the University of Mississippi (Ole Miss) campus is known for parking BMWs up close to the front door. Therefore when the rushees approach the house, they are either impressed or intimidated. But, as you know, some people can fake it, and make it work for them. Appearances will be important to these girls. This house is filled with bloodlines and family jewels. Known as the "old money" house, these sisters are well dressed and connected. This house may seem a bit stuffy at first, but give it a thorough look. Remember: Not all of these sisters are wealthy, just enough to give the house its reputation.

Delta Delta Delta, Formal, University of Kentucky, 1959

Beautiful Barbie

A Georgia house is notorious for the fragrant blends of Chanel perfume and Vidal Sassoon shampoo, amidst an abundance of Laura Ashley designs. There is a beauty queen house on every campus and these young ladies keep the Clinique stock thriving. There will most likely be a Miss Virginia or Miss Ohio standing out front to welcome you as you come through the front door. Beauty, bathing suit measurements, and wardrobe go a long way at this house.

These are the girls who don't meet up with friends on a Saturday night. If they don't have a date, they don't go out. They may stay at home with their other dateless Cinderella sisters, work out with their recently purchased exercise equipment, order in low-fat takeout (never pizza), and relax to music while trading pedicures and facials.

What a life! It sure beats braving those dateless Saturday nights alone. When it comes to the major events (homecoming, formals), these girls always have dates. Big sisters look out for their little sisters and set them up on blind dates with some of their fraternity friends. They are usually the toasts of the town, in that it is a status symbol for a guy to be seen with a girl from a beauty queen sorority.

Academic Annie

Think Hillary Rodham Clinton, think Barbara Walters. This is a think, think, think kind of house. An A on a mid-term statistics test is a far greater feat than getting a date to the homecoming game. Armed with ambition and brains, these no-nonsense intellectuals have little time for television. They're too busy discussing the theory of evolution. There is always a challenging conversation to be had and these congresswomen of tomorrow are forever looking for ways to better the environment, the country, the world. Politically correct, these sisters are usually premed or prelaw and have taken over a wing in the campus library. To be invited here, you'll probably need a high school grade point average of 3.25 or higher. If stimulating intelligent conversation is your idea of fun, then welcome home. During Rush, while visiting this house, if words are used that you don't understand and political conversations float around your head leaving you dizzy and speechless, get out.

This is probably not the best house for you, although four years can change anyone. Any ambitious young lady is capable of learning anything.

Partying Patty

This is the house full of girls who are always up for a good time. While academics and world politics are not often discussed, the sisters in this house can always tell you who the newest "in" band is or where the best frat parties are. These girls are usually very genuine and nice, but the savviest girls in the house know how to establish a happy medium between party-hearty and making the grades. After all, you are in college to learn something, as well as to have a good time. This laid-back sorority could be just the place for you if you can keep yourself focused on school during the week and the party scene only on weekends. If you pledge here, try to find a big sis who can help you establish the happy medium—and it could work out great!

Fit Frannie

Whether it is flag football, soccer,

tennis, or golf, these sisters are always up for the challenge. Embodying the strength and fitness of Olympiads, this house prevails in intramural sports and is proud of it. Good health, eating balanced diets, working out, and natural beauty are characteristics of this progressive house. Running shorts, sweatshirts, and tennis shoes are the standard dress code here. Fresh faces, little make-up, and muscular calves are all stand-outs. The competitive rushee who enjoys athletic activities and sports tournaments will be right at home here.

Perky Pamela

The smell of fresh cookies is rising from this kitchen. Photographs of the sisters helping elderly women cross the street line the halls, along with awards for picking up trash in the park and fundraising to save the whales. These sisters have never met a cause they weren't for or a problem they couldn't solve. Clear headed and good hearted, this sorority participates in endless charities throughout the year. Your involvement in this house could help others and benefit you in the meantime. Not only will you feel good about what

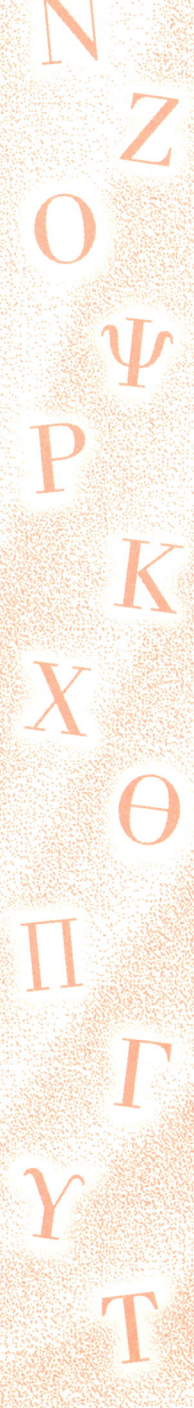

you are doing, you will also have a great time sharing these experiences with your new sisters. If social work and helping others are your goals, take a close look at this house.

Natural Nancy

Tie-dyed shirts, ripped jeans, and Birkenstocks are the standard attire in this free-spirited sorority. These girls believe in the au naturel look. They take long hikes and practice yoga. The sixties are alive and well here. Rock and roll and laid-back attitudes are common here, yet commitment to equal rights and liberal politics are inevitable. This house is probably less judgmental than some others. While they don't fit the stereotype of the typical sorority girl, these young women may turn up anywhere from a fraternity formal to a political rally. You just never know what they will do next.

Mixture Molly

Although these profiles may seem a bit extreme, you can bet there is one on every campus. Ideally you will find a sorority that fits your personality. If you do not fit into one of these profiles, never fear—look for the sorority that thrives on diversity. There is always one house that prides itself with having all types of personalities as members. They welcome young women from brainy to beautiful, and everyone in between. Everyone here has her own opinion, and you must be a self-assured young woman in order to fit in. This house is a lively and educational place to hang your hat. With so many different personality types, there is always something brewing. This house is a lot of fun, but be careful. With so many personality types under one roof, it can be a hot bed for controversy. Rushees with good self esteem, who don't fit into any particular mold, might make this their happy new home.

SISTER TALK

When my little sister went through Rush at the University of Mississippi (Ole Miss) some twenty years after I did, I was thrilled to recommend my sorority, Pi Beta Phi (Pi Phi), to her for one main reason: the variety and

quality of women who were my sisters. The Pi Phi I experienced in 1979 to 1983 did not exist as a sorority with only members from Mississippi who all looked alike, talked alike, and dated alike. Sure, we had some wonderful Mississippians, but we also had Houston sisters, New Orleans sisters (Mardi Gras!), Alabama sisters, Arkansas sisters, Memphis sisters, Florida sisters, California sisters, Rhode Island sisters, and so on. In addition to the geographic diversity, we had drill team members, cheerleaders, campus politicos, newspaper editors, tennis players, pharmacy majors, premed majors, education majors, finance majors, wild girls, shy girls—you get the picture.

My sister called me the night before she pledged to tell me that she felt more at home with another group than she did with my sorority. "Go for it," I advised her. "You're the one who's joining this time around, not me. The fit needs to be right for you." And I'm happy to say that it is. My sister knew early in the process that she felt more comfortable, more like herself, and more likely to find kindred spirits at the Alpha Omicron Pi house than the others she visited. Like this book says, that house "shone through like a beacon" for her. And that's what "going Greek" is all about.

To sum it up, during my years at Ole Miss, the Pi Phis were a really great group of all different types of women. Because I consider myself an individual, not one to follow others just for the sake of following, I'm still thankful that I wasn't part of a conformist group. Being encouraged to be myself while being accepted by a larger community serves me well even today. And I'm sure the same will be true for my sister.

Lee Ann Mayo
B.B.A., M.B.A., vice-president,
marketing research company

CHAPTER 5 CHECKLIST

- ☑ *Before Rush begins, research the reputation of each sorority on campus. Don't take the reputations too literally, however. Each house has many different personalities as a part of its whole.*
- ☑ *Seek out the house that you feel most comfortable with, regardless of what those around you might think.*
- ☑ *Keep an open mind about each house.*

NOTES

NOTES

CHAPTER 6

Is That What You're Wearing?

We've all heard our mothers—or our boyfriends—ask that question. And we hate to say it, but it's true during Rush as well. Remember, you're in your late teens, not your mid twenties. High fashion and current fads are exciting to look at if you're strolling Fifth Avenue in New York or thumbing through the latest issue of your favorite magazine. But it's a bit much for Rush. Fashion designers often use gray, black, charcoal, or navy. We recommend rushees stay away from these dark colors. Your tailored black

Alpha Omicron Pi, Bid Day, University of Kentucky, 1998

suit is better for that first round of job interviews after completing your third year of law school than it is for sorority Rush. If Rush is in August, you'll want to give the impression that you are fresh and crisp. Light, breezy colors and fabrics will set the tone for the happy rushee. We're not suggesting that you wear a floral print that looks more like your grandmother's parlor drapes than a suitable, smart dress; but we are suggesting that you experiment with pastels. Of course if Rush is in January, you'll want to alter your wardrobe as appropriate for the winter season.

The dress code varies from campus to campus. Consult the Rush brochure from your school to see if you're allowed to wear shorts or sundresses. Once you know the dress code, go on a shopping outing where all you do is look. Try colors that you've never worn before, and take an honest friend who can help you decipher what colors bring out your eyes, work well with your skin tones, and help illuminate your own individual beauty. Be sure to include comfortable shoes that match your various outfits. You'll be on your feet a lot, so leave the high heels at home for now! Keep in mind, the sororities are looking for original and unique—not odd or showy.

There's nothing more refreshing than an active meeting a new person during Rush and being able to report to the others that she met such a "neat girl." As brief as these ten-minute conversations are, what you had on is often how you are described to the sisters at the evening round-up meeting. "Did you meet Cindy Jones?" A confused sister may respond, "I'm not sure, what was she wearing?" As you get further into the process and get to know the girls at the various houses, the wardrobe will certainly become less important. But as with most things in life, first impressions are important and lasting. And you only get one chance to make a first impression.

Family Jewels

Jewelry, as any well-dressed woman will tell you, can make or break an outfit. We recommend that you keep it simple during Rush. Even if you're lucky enough to have diamonds or emeralds, you don't have to impress anyone with expensive jewels. A wardrobe essential for sisters of all ages, from pledges to alums, is a simple pair of pearl earrings. Pearl earrings are dainty and feminine, and they go with everything. They're also

For more information:

NATIONAL PANHELLENIC CONFERENCE
3901 W. 86th St., Suite 380
Indianapolis, IN 46268
(317) 872-3185

affordable. You can find a nice pair of pearl earrings at any of the discount jewelry houses or many department stores in your local mall. The actives certainly cannot tell the difference from the discount house pearls and those bought in the elegant pearl district of Japan. And although it's not needed, a special strand of pearls for preference night is definitely a nice touch. (Maybe you can borrow your mom's!) Keep in mind that even before you walk through the door, the actives in the house know a lot about you, so you don't need to resort to overkill.

We recommend that you stay away from trendy jewelry. Dangling earrings, clunky bracelets, and faddish necklaces are a waste of money. You don't want the actives distracted by your jewelry, so if it's not subtle, don't wear it, and if you can't afford simple gold hoops or basic pearls, don't wear any. While going through Rush, as in most of life, less is more, so let the natural you shine through.

Hair Essentials

All of us have experienced bad hair days. When you're walking around in the warm sun, going from house to house, bad hair has a tendency to be every day, all day long, during Rush. To avoid those bad hair days, a blunt cut is a smart way to go. Crisp hairstyles are fashionable and carry the aura of a confident young woman. The days of big hair, tressled locks, and teasing are over. Thank goodness! If you have a long, beautiful mane, make sure your ends are blunt. If you use color, keep in mind the

Kappa Kappa Gamma, Bid Day, University of Kentucky, 1988

rule of thumb that subtle is better.

If you need highlights to enhance a bland blonde, by all means do it, but select a colorist carefully and make sure when you walk out the door into the bright sunlight that your new do looks natural. A good colorist can weave in hues of soft golds and gentle reds. If it takes the colorist three hours, it's well worth it. Real sophistication and class come from natural beauty. If your hair color does not flatter you, by all means cheat; just don't make it obvious. If you are already an elevated blonde or a tinted brunette helped along by your favorite colorist, don't show your roots. Although showing roots is a trend that has swept Hollywood starlets and high-fashion models, it is only a trend. A rushee is not going for the disheveled, cooler than ice look. You're a lady, and you want the very essence of you to radiate.

Hands On

Ever asked a blushing bride on the most important day of her life to see her set and when she proudly shows off her rings, you can't get past her chewed off nails? Well, it's not exactly the most important time of your life, but Rush week is single-handedly the beginning of the next four years of your life—a crucial period for you. Manicured nails are of paramount importance for the finished look. Stay away from gaudy, eye-catching colors. Gentle pinks and pastels are safe, and a French manicure offers a clean look. Nails that are too long are just as much of a turnoff as bad nails. If you don't have time for a manicure, make sure your nails are clean and filed. One more thing: Avoid too many rings. One on each hand is best.

Remember, less is more!

SISTER TALK

When I left my hometown, bound for the University of Kentucky, I was confident that I would become a Tri Delt (Delta Delta Delta), just like my mother. When Rush began and I entered the Tri Delt house, I was overcome with reverence and wonder. After all, my mother had lived here. Was she as nervous then as I was now?

In a display of bravado, I inquired about their philanthropic activities on campus, and the history of the chapter, but what I really wanted to see was the room where my mother had lived. Maybe then I would feel a sense of certitude that was missing. After all, I belonged here, didn't I?

As I went from house to house, I began to think that maybe I did not belong anywhere. Then I went to the Kappa Kappa Gamma (Kappa) house. Suddenly, the girls ran out of the house and filled the air with so much energy that I forgot about the heat, the humidity, and the Tri Delt house.

The first person to greet me was the house mother. Her joie de vivre was contagious. I liked her immediately. In fact, I liked everything about Kappa. Upstairs was a map of the world with pins placed in the states and countries that were represented by the members of the sorority. What I remember most was the enthusiasm and vitality of the members. It was infectious.

When the party was over, I left with a smile on my face. This was where I belonged.

Although I knew I wanted to be a Kappa, I was torn by the desire to wear my mother's Tri Delt pin. What was I to do? Should I pledge Tri Delt and just make the best of it? To my surprise, I was cut by Tri Delt before Preference Night. I remember my Rush counselor asking me how I felt. Was I upset? Yes and no. I was disappointed that Momma would not be there to place her pin on me, but thrilled that I could pledge Kappa and perhaps start a legacy of my own.

Mary Smock
B.A., M.A., high school teacher

CHAPTER 6 CHECKLIST

- ☑ *Keep clothing tasteful and appropriate. Bear in mind the seasons.*
- ☑ *Make sure every item is altered properly, ironed, and ready to go.*
- ☑ *Wear comfortable, clean shoes.*
- ☑ *Choose simple, not showy, jewelry.*
- ☑ *Style your hair in a well-kept and neat fashion.*
- ☑ *Clean and trim nails or get a manicure.*
- ☑ *Buy extra pantyhose or tights—just in case!*

NOTES

NOTES

CHAPTER 7

Etiquette Essentials

Before you set foot through the door, the actives know a lot about you already. To register for Rush, contact the campus Panhellenic Office and they will send you a detailed form, known as the Panhellenic Recruitment Week Registration Form. This form asks for information, such as where you went to high school, your graduation date, your grade point average, family sorority affiliation (if any), honors, activities, and community service. You are the person who is responsible for filling out this form and this is not the time to be shy or modest about your accomplishments. This is the time to brag, just a little, without

To sign up for Rush, contact the panhellenic office at your school as soon as possible!

being boastful. If you haven't quite fulfilled your goals and personal dreams in high school, don't let on. Put a positive spin on any accomplishment. Chances are, it will sound great. Make a commitment to yourself that you're going to make up for all your missed opportunities in the next four years. You can do it!

On the Other Side

Rush varies from campus to campus, but usually during the first round, or *open house*, as it is sometimes called, you will be offered something nonalcoholic to drink. As you go through the second and third rounds, you might be offered light snacks at each house. Some universities are going to a *no frills Rush*, meaning no food or elaborate drinks. Regardless of your school's format, be sure to start each day with a healthy breakfast and lunch. This is not the time to go on that crash diet! From personal experience, we can say that a hungry rushee does not make the best impression. Stimulating conversation can be difficult when your stomach sounds like a freight train.

If you are a little clumsy, or if you seem to have three feet when you get nervous, practice high tea before Rush week. Go to a favorite coffee house or deli and sip tea and have finger sandwiches with a pal before Rush begins. Don't overdo the ladylike eating skills, just make sure your punch doesn't wind up in your lap or worse—in an active's lap!

A surefire way to get yourself cut from a house is to go in with gum in your mouth. If you want to go on a suicide mission, smoke a cigarette and put it out as you're walking up the front lawn. These are two absolute unladylike actions that any house will notice and remember. Anyway, smoking is bad for you, and we bet your mother taught you not to chew gum in public anyway. So just consider this a polite reminder.

And Now Introducing…

The manner in which you introduce yourself will set the tone for the few minutes that you spend with the actives. When an active approaches you, smile and make eye contact. If she doesn't introduce herself, take the initiative by offering your hand and saying, "Hello, I'm Elizabeth Stern and I don't believe we've met." The active will introduce herself and probably begin to lead the conversation. If her conversational skills are not up to par, offer her a small but honest compliment. "This is a beautiful home," will work, but try to focus on something more personal, like "I love your earrings." Maybe this will lead into a story about where she purchased them or who gave them to her. Before you know it, chances are you will have spent ten minutes with an active who has told you her life's story. Showing interest in others marks you as a confident person. Studies show that

Chi Omega, Bid Day, University of Mississippi, 1979

people who have conversations in which they are given the opportunity to speak primarily about themselves tend to have fond feelings for the person who prompted the conversation.

Say Cheese!

Have you ever wanted to draw positive attention to yourself? That can be accomplished instantly and it will be the single most importance thing that you can do during Rush. The best part is that anyone can do it and it doesn't cost a cent. All you have to do is open your mouth and turn up the corners of your lips. See how easy it is! You have heard it over and over, but you really can set the world on fire with a smile. (Our mother still tells us this all the time!)

Before you walk into a house, recount a happy memory. That first kiss from the hunk in high school or winning the state track meet—whatever puts a genuine smile on your face and a warm spot in your heart will do the trick. Give yourself a few seconds to relive that moment and you will suddenly be in a good mood. You will radiate happiness and everyone likes to be around an upbeat person. It makes them feel good, too.

SISTER TALK

My experience with Alpha Omicron Pi (AOII) in college taught me leadership skills, which enabled me to perform other offices in community and church organizations. It taught me to always strive for excellence and to never back down from my beliefs.

After moving to Nashville with my husband from Memphis, I was in search for some new friends. So I got involved with the Nashville alumnae chapter and began to network with new AOII sisters. About a year later, I heard of the opening for Conference Administrator at AOII headquarters. After working in the hotel industry for six years and utilizing the skills I learned in college, now I was going to give back to AOII by planning their trainings and conventions.

Being an AOII staff member has given me a new perspective about AOII. It is exciting to see a group of women on staff from all different age groups work together for a common goal. Just as we would do in our philanthropy efforts in school, we now strive to provide collegiate and alumnae chapters with the very best programming that will further their knowledge in school and in their careers so they will be able to give something back to their campuses and

Delta Delta Delta, Rush, University of Kentucky, 1978

communities. We really are a volunteer driven organization. The skills that AOII teaches in school will carry with you for the rest of your life.

Angela Mills
B.A., association executive

CHAPTER 7 CHECKLIST

- ☑ *Polish your etiquette and social skills before Rush begins.*
- ☑ *Use your best manners.*
- ☑ *No smoking or chewing gum!*
- ☑ *Offer your hand for a firm handshake and introduce yourself.*
- ☑ *Give a realistic compliment to the active.*
- ☑ *Show sincere interest in the conversation.*
- ☑ *Establish eye contact.*
- ☑ *Smile!*

NOTES

NOTES

CHAPTER 8

First Things First

Go into each sorority house ready to share and chat. Sorority girls are big on talk and are known for conversing about almost anything. A surefire way to guarantee yourself a good conversationalist is to be abreast of current issues. Watch the news every day and read the newspaper. Stay up on fashion and designers, peruse a couple of best-selling books, be aware of the latest trends in nutrition, and even if your summer was as boring as burned toast, have an interesting topic in reserve for discussion. You might even be able to entertain yourself during one of those lulls in the conversation, which will happen eventually.

A good conversationalist is self-confident, perceptive, *and* a good listener. She can initiate interesting topics and read reactions and feelings from others. A successful conversationalist is intelligent and knows how to make others feel at ease. "The gift of the gab" is usually found in people who honestly want to make others feel good, and they usually have a keen sense of humor. They know when to lighten the conversation with an appropriate joke. People seem to gravitate toward such able individuals.

Regardless of how funny you are or how perceptive, if you use poor judgment in your conversation topics you will bomb. Bad language or off-colored stories are huge negatives, not only during Rush, but always. Don't offer the latest gossip you've heard or criticize other sororities. This will only make you look bad. Avoid any mention of boys—especially old boyfriends. You never know who has been out with whom, or if the jerk you dated two years ago is the precious younger brother of an active. Nothing good can come from the topic of boys in this situation. Save it for your late-night gab sessions with close friends. Instead, focus on such safe subjects as current events, adjusting to college life, and personal goals. Show a

TOP TEN THINGS YOU SHOULD NOT SAY AT A RUSH PARTY

1. "I hear the guys on campus call this house the kennel!"

2. "Every girl here has the exact same hair color!"

3. "My mother was a XYZ and my sister was XYZ, so I'm just killing time here at ABC."

4. "This house is my fourth choice."

5. "Doesn't anyone here believe in deodorant?"

6. "Are those brownies fat free? If so, you can't tell it by looking at the actives."

7. "If I pledge this house, will there be room upstairs for my pet python?"

8. "Hey, I have a great dermatologist I can recommend for you."

9. "And I thought I had big hips! If I pledge here I'll bring along my workout tapes."

10. "Most of the other actives are snobby, but you seem okay."

genuine interest in the conversation by making eye contact and relying on natural expressions.

Brush up on your English if you don't feel comfortable with your language skills. Poor grammar, slang, and swear words are red flags for actives. A good vocabulary can make the dullest story seem like climbing Mt. Everest if worded colorfully. It's not only what you say, but also how you say it that counts.

Being a social butterfly is hard work. For every active you meet, try to remember her name and one key topic that you discussed with her. Use the active's name in the conversation at least three times. If you repeat a person's name while speaking with her, you are more likely to remember it later.

Once you remember her name, you then need to remember something about her so the next time you see her you can bring up a subject that interests her. We recommend keeping a small notepad in your purse. After each party, take a few minutes to make notes about the house and the actives you met. (Do this discreetly—not in front of lots of people!) List each active's name and everything you can remember about your conversation. Write your honest feelings and instincts about the sorority.

At the end of each round, the sororities tend to blur into one. These notes will help you to remember your feelings about each house.

On the Other Side

The actives arrive on campus ten days to two weeks before Rush begins to spruce up the house for Rush and to get to know everything they can about you. During this working week, sororities practice skits and rotations, where actives hand off one another to meet the maximum number of rushees. They also have rushee sessions in which they painstakingly go over each girl for whom they have a recommendation. They memorize the name, face, legacies, and activities of those rushees with recs. These are the rushees that the alumnae or actives have personally pointed out for the sorority to take a good look at. Several Kappa Kappa Gamma alumnae at Vanderbilt University sent Goo-Goo Clusters to the Kappas at the University of Virginia campus. Wrapped around each candy bar was a ribbon that read, "Vandy alumnae are Goo-Goo over Laura Smith and Cheryl Wood!" This not only fed the

Kappa Alpha Theta, Duke University, 1974

actives a tasty treat but also made everyone remember these two rushees. Needless to say, both Laura and Cheryl pledged Kappa Kappa Gamma.

Don't be surprised if an active calls you by name and asks you about your lifeguarding job before you tell her where you worked over the summer. They have memorized everything about you that appeared on the recommendation, as well as your face from that all-important picture. Again, we cannot overemphasize the importance of completed recommendations and appropriate photographs.

While we are on the topic of pictures, be careful what you send. Rushees commonly become know by nicknames from these photos and are jokingly referred to in this shorthand over the next few weeks. We remember a rushee known as "Bozo" because of her bright polka-dot dress with a big collar. Our personal favorite was "Miss January," who made the mistake of submitting an all-too-revealing photo for the entire sorority to view.

RUSHEE'S BILL OF RIGHTS

- The right to be treated as an individual.
- The right to be fully informed about the Rush process.
- The rights to ask questions and receive true and objective answers from Rush counselors and sorority members.
- The right to be treated with respect.
- The right to be treated as a capable and mature person without being patronized.
- The right to ask how and why and receive straight answers.
- The right to have and express opinions to Rush counselors.
- The right to have inviolable confidentiality when sharing information with Rush counselors.
- The right to make informed choices without undue pressure from others.
- The right to be fully informed about the binding agreements implicit in the preference card signing.
- The rights to make one's own choice and decision and accept full responsibility for the results of that decision.
- The right to have a positive, safe, and enriching Rush and pledging experience.

NATIONAL PANHELLENIC CONFERENCE

SISTER TALK

I wasn't sure I wanted to join a sorority, but my father really wanted me to go through Rush because he had been in a fraternity in college and neither of my sisters or my mother had gone to schools that had Greek systems. I think my father's experience had been a positive one. He was a Sigma Chi at Davidson in the late 1940s and he wanted to share that with me. Rush was deferred at Southern Methodist University in Dallas, so I had a whole semester to consider it. It didn't take long to realize that the people who were in sororities and fraternities seemed to be having more fun than those who weren't (i.e., a fuller social calendar). With a student body that was at least 50% Greek, most of the people I knew were Greek.

In the end, my final decision was sort of a spiritual one. There were a handful of girls in the Kappa Kappa Gamma house who really loved the Lord, and somehow they found out that faith was important to me. Those girls made sure I knew that I'd have fellowship in their house—Bible studies, women of like minds, etc. Once I pledged, however, I found out that it was a pretty wild house, with the exception of those few girls! So it took me a little while to find my spot, but I did. And I made some really great friends—two in particular—whom I otherwise wouldn't have known. From a social perspective, it certainly enhanced my college experience. I loved parties, formals, etc., and there were always plenty of those things happening (sounds pretty shallow for the girl who pledged for spiritual reasons, but, alas, it's true!). And, not to be overlooked, I ate well. The cooks at the Kappa house were terrific—certainly an improvement over cafeteria fare. Also, the house was so warm and inviting, it was a real home away from home for me. Lastly, it gave me a sense of identity on campus. As unfair as this sounds, some associations were made by which sorority or fraternity you joined. I was lucky to have chosen a good one. Even if I did feel like a "lone ranger" at times because of my religious beliefs—a feeling I experienced in other environments as well, not just the sorority house—being in a sorority helped me learn to get along with and forge relationships with girls who had a different set of values and interests than I did.

Mary Bailey
B.F.A., magazine editor, wife, and mother of two

CHAPTER 8 CHECKLIST

- ✓ Contact the Panhellenic Office at your school to inquire about Rush as soon as you are admitted.
- ✓ Be aware of current events, movies, and fashion for good conversation topics.
- ✓ Be a good listener.
- ✓ Uncover the other person's interests and focus on those.
- ✓ Have a light-hearted joke on standby for lulls in conversation.
- ✓ Use proper grammar.
- ✓ Avoid the subject of boys!
- ✓ Repeat a person's name often during the conversation.
- ✓ Make notes after leaving the house.
- ✓ Don't be surprised if the actives know your name. They have spent hours and hours going through the recs and registration forms.

NOTES

NOTES

CHAPTER 9

Showtime!

Consult your university's Rush schedule and be familiar with how many rounds comprise the Rush period. Although the number of rounds varies from campus to campus, there are usually three to five, with the latter parties becoming more serious, longer, and more formal. *REMEMBER: Although the format may differ from that discussed in the following sections, the process is similar at most schools.*

When you arrive on campus you will be assigned a Rush group. This is the group of girls that you will attend the first group of parties with. Your Rush group will be your family for the next several days. Everyone in your group is in the same heart-wrenching position that you are. They are all just as scared and nervous, so try to relax and make some new friends. (One of our friends met a girl in her Rush group who became her best college friend, and they both pledged Chi Omega together.)

Each group is assigned a Rush counselor, known as a *Rho Chi*, who will act as your surrogate mother for the next week. Rho Chi's are Greek women who have unaffiliated themselves from their houses during Rush week. They cannot reveal to you or any other rushee their sorority affiliation. And they are forbidden to speak to their sisters. This is so you will feel free to discuss all sororities with your Rush counselor without feeling like you would hurt her feelings if you did not pledge her house or that she might tell her sisters your true feelings. The Rush counselor cannot speak to any of her sisters during Rush week, so do not feel she is for or against you pledging her house. She is there to answer your questions, help you find your way around campus, wipe the tears, and share in the joy. Rush counselors have a tough, yet rewarding job. They are the ones who bring you your invitations and take your acceptances back to the houses. They see heartbreak and elation. They are mother,

JANE PAULEY LOOKS BACK

"One memory of Rush stands out: the Kappa Kappa Gamma house seemed so sophisticated to my freshman eyes and I was very self-consciously unsophisticated. When an upperclassman asked me if I liked [artist] Toulouse-Lautrec, I replied, truthfully, 'all I know about Toulouse-Lautrec is that he was short!' She laughed out loud and evidently told everyone I was very funny. Lesson: don't fret over your weaknesses, just play to your strengths—self-deprecating humor has always been my forte."

JANE PAULEY
journalist, broadcaster, and television personality

counselor, and friend.

Each university has Rush rules. Make yourself aware of the rules and be sure to obey them. The *silence rule* is common on most campuses. Enforced from the beginning of Rush until Bid Day, there is to be no communication between rushees and rushing actives except during Rush parties. This means if your biological sister is in a sorority on campus and you are going through Rush, you cannot communicate with her except when you see each other at scheduled parties. Although this may seem extreme, it is intended to be in your best interest. By not receiving phone calls and visits from Greek women, you are free to make your own decision with the least amount of pressure as possible.

Never skip a party that you are scheduled to attend. This not only reflects poorly on you, but you could also be disqualified from Rush. If you become ill or have an emergency, contact your Rho Chi immediately. She will notify the necessary people and possibly reschedule for you. Once you have met your Rush group and Rush counselor, you are ready to begin. Your Rush counselor will give you your schedule for the first round of parties. Study it, know where you are supposed to be when, and put on a smile.

Round One

Open house. Meet and greet. Fast-paced, big smiles, high energy. Actives sing their sorority theme songs outside on the lawn. You'll be swept through as many as six houses a day. The actives will say hello, give you a brief tour of the house, and acquaint themselves with you. Many houses prefer you to bring a tea card with your name printed on it so they have a record of your attendance. Have these cards printed before Rush. As you walk through the front door, you will be introduced to the sorority president, the sorority Rush chairmen, and then handed off to an active in line. We'll call her Missy.

Missy will show you around the house for a few minutes and then, out of the blue, Joanie will show up, anxious to meet you. Missy will then excuse herself to let the two of you get to know each other. A handoff of this nature will take place two or three times during this party so that you will be able to meet several different actives. This is called *rotation*, and actives have it

Approximately three million women have embraced the sorority experience since the 1800s.

down to a science. It is practiced and perfected during "work week," the week that actives spend in preparation for Rush before you even arrive.

This is where preplanned fresh and probing questions will come in handy. The actives are geared and ready to chat, but they are not robots and there will be lulls in the conversation. Keep in mind that many first-year actives are just as nervous as you are. Now is the time to ask questions about the house, what they represent as a chapter, or their big sister-little sister program. Ask about their involvement with intramural sports and their scholastic strengths. Avoid asking about financial requirements or dropping alumnae names. It is not ladylike to discuss money, and if you're close with an alumna or active, let them tell the house about you. It's more impressive that way!

Be sure to answer questions with lively, interesting responses and avoid one-word answers, which can halt conversation. Try to ask the actives with whom you speak open-ended questions, and avoid yes/no questions. This allows the actives to tell you about themselves and their feelings about the sorority. The more information you gather, the better able you'll be to make an appropriate decision when the time comes. It also helps the time to fly by if you are having interesting conversations with involved actives. (Check the end of this chapter for some great sample Rush questions.)

A Round One party is a whirlwind lasting from 30 minutes to 1 hour. Then you'll be off to another house. Remember to have your notepad handy when you leave. Make notes about the women you met, reminders about the house, and any conversation topics you covered. Be sure to do this discreetly, once you have left the house. Some things to consider include how you felt when you walked through the door, whether or not you are interested in getting to know the women better, and the friendliness of the actives.

Immediately after you leave the house, the actives in the rotation gather and discuss you and the other rushees they met. They review each of the six or seven girls in their group and decide whether to ask them back; put them up for discussion; or decline to invite them back. Unless you've had an unpleasant experience, you'll want to be invited back. But keep in mind that this decision is made under severe time constraints. Do not get your feelings hurt if you do not receive a second invitation to every house.

Every night after Round One, the actives go over their party lists and discuss the rushees. Most sororities use the block voting method. There are three lists of girls read aloud or distributed. The first list is the girls that are recommended by the rotation groups to be invited back for Round Two. If a name is read that an active feels should not be issued an invitation, she moves to have that rushee moved to the discussion list. After all the questionable names have been removed, this list is voted on as a block. The rushees on this list will be invited for Round Two.

Next comes the list of rushees that were not recommended to be invited back by the actives that met them at the party. Just like the first list, this group of names is read aloud. Like before, if an active would like to have a name removed from this list, she asks to move the rushee over to the "open for discussion" list. When all actives are satisfied with the names on the "no invite" list, it is voted on as a block and those rushees will not be invited back.

Now is when the real work begins for actives. The list of rushees who are on the "open for discussion" list is read. Here's the chance for one of your friends who may already be an active to save you from the "no invite" list. She will stand up and say what a terrific girl you are and that you must have been overlooked. On the other hand, an active that is scorned or has some bad information on a rushee is encouraged to use dignity and grace when discussing the rushee in public. She will probably use abbreviated phrases such as "happy elsewhere." This is an understood code for "I don't think she'd be the best sister for us." Unless there is another active there to counter this assertion, the sorority will take the active's word and decline to invite the rushee back.

This session can be emotional and heated. A few years ago, Jane, a friend of our friend Mary, was going through Rush at Tulane in New Orleans. Much to Mary's dismay, she found out that Jane was on the "no invite" list of her own sorority house by the girls who had met her during Round One. Mary stood up in tears at this session and pointed out that rushee Jane was not only a great student but was also going to be a Tulane cheerleader, a visible and active position that none of the current sisters held. Needless to say, the sisters realized that this girl was worth a second look. Jane went on to be the president of her pledge class.

Unfortunately, many sorority sisters get their feelings hurt and have friends cut during this session. Terri, who pledged Kappa Delta her freshman year at the University of Alabama, found out how rough Rush can be on the other side her first year as an active. Rebecca,

RUSH WEEK MUST HAVE CHECKLIST

- **Umbrella**—This is not the time for the wet puppy look!

- **Tea cards**—The ones from your high school graduation invitations will do.

- **Comfortable shoes**—Happy feet make happy rushees.

- **Watch**—A tardy rushee is a cut rushee.

- **Small notepad**—Make sure this will fit in the purses you will be carrying to the parties.

- **Small cash/change**—You never know when you might need to make a phone call or a small purchase.

- A copy of *Ready for Rush!*—An informed rushee is soon to be a pledge!

one of her friends, was going through Rush as a sophomore. During the cut session, Terri discovered Rebecca's name on the "no invite" list. She stood up and gave a passionate speech about how she had known Rebecca throughout their freshman year and thought she would be a real asset to the group. After her speech, Terri was asked to leave the room so the actives could openly discuss Rebecca without hurting Terri's feelings. While she was out of earshot, several other actives stood up and said they also knew Rebecca from freshman year and considered her reputation to be questionable. This came down to which active the other actives trusted the most. Due to the questionable reputation factor, Rebecca was not invited back. Terri left the house in tears that night. Not only did she feel that she let Rebecca down, she was also angry at her sisters. So don't feel like the actives have it easy. Rush is difficult no matter which side you're on.

After Round One, a large number of the rushees are cut. Round One is often the harshest cut and it is generally based on first appearance and what they know about you. Many sororities do their grades cut after this party. This is when any rushee without the required

GPA is automatically not invited back. This GPA is determined by each sorority's national headquarters and varies from sorority to sorority.

When each sorority has finished its voting session, they submit their invitation list to the campus Panhellenic Council. The council then issues invitations for each rushee on behalf of each sorority. This is where you get to do the choosing. You will meet with your Rush counselor to review the invitations you received. You then choose to accept a predetermined number of invitations and these are the houses you will visit for Round Two. You may have been invited back to every sorority or you may only get a few invitations. Look at your choices with an honest and open mind. Choose to accept the sororities that really feel right for you. Don't be offended if you get cut from any particular one. Count it as a blessing and focus your energy on a house that is more suitable for you.

Keep in mind that you are under no obligation to join a sorority. Rush is the opportunity for you to visit the sororities, get a glimpse of Greek life, and assess whether you would like to be a part of the Greek community. But if you receive a bid and decide not to accept it, you will not be able to participate in Rush again for one calendar year.

Round Two

If invited back, you'll get to know more about the sorority. It's still light and breezy during Round Two, but conversations will be longer and you'll begin to get a sense of what the house is about. You will be attending several of these parties a day, and they last longer than those in Round One. Review your notes on each sorority before you walk through the door. Remember the names, faces, and interests of the actives you met during Round One. The rotation process will begin again. You will see some of the girls you met at the first party, but you will meet many new girls as well.

After the "chat session," each house will put on a skit that will show why their house is special. These skits are entertaining and lighthearted. They range from spins on popular television shows and Broadway plays, to imitating themselves. Be attentive to the skits and laugh and smile no matter how corny or sappy they are. The actives are watching the rushees for their reactions

Check out the Web for various sorority sites and for more information on college life and Greek life in general.

and no smile might be interpreted as a bored or disinterested rushee. This is a fine line to walk, because a fake is more of a turnoff than a bore. Try to relax, smile, and enjoy yourself. Hopefully you won't have to fake it too much! Don't forget to take notes after you leave, focusing on your comfort level with these women and your impression of their involvement with campus activities. Did they seem sincere? Were you

relaxed? Does this sorority emphasize academics, athletics, and/or outreach enough to satisfy you?

Each night after Round Two, while you're out having Chinese food with other Rush hopefuls or hanging out with your new friends in the dorm, the

Sample Rush Questions

For those awkward lulls in conversation, have questions ready! Here are a few suggestions for you to ask the actives.

- Why did you pledge this house?
- How do you encourage scholarship?
- What kind of social activities is this chapter involved in?
- Do you have strong community relationships?
- What philanthropies does this house support?
- Am I obligated to live a certain number of years in the sorority house?
- What is your favorite part of being in this sorority?
- How do you get your big sister?
- Do you have a close relationship with your big sister?

actives are in long, late-night hash sessions. They're going over the parties of the day, talking about you and the other rushees they met, and trying to zero in on the right pledges for them. During the "open for discussion" list, a process called *dissension* or *2-2-1* begins. For each rushee discussed, two positive things are said and then two negative things. Each discussion ends with one positive thing said. (Every school may have a different method. We know of several sororities that do not require actives to say something negative about rushees.) This helps the actives look at the pros and cons of pledging a particular girl. The "positives" could be anything from "great hair" to "4.0 G.P.A.," and the "negatives" could be "tacky purse" to "questionable reputation." This gives actives a measuring stick as to if there is any real reason not to have the rushee as a sister or if someone is just being petty. The "hash sessions" or "cut sessions" can be long and tedious, often lasting far past midnight. The block voting method is used again. More discussion takes place during this voting session. Not just anyone gets invited back after this party. The actives start to ask themselves, "Can I see her as my sister?" If the answer is no, you will not be invited back. But if the answer is yes, you are one step closer.

You will receive invitations to Round Three after this round of parties. Once again you will meet with your Rush counselor to go over your invitations and to narrow your acceptances down even more. Slowly but surely, your list is getting shorter, and so is theirs.

Round Three

If you've been invited back for Round Three, the house is definitely interested in pledging you. They've seen you twice now. Past the initial stage, they're not inviting you back just to fill up their house for the party! They are genuinely interested in you and now's your time to shine. The third round is the longest party, lasting up to two hours. Study your notes on each house and try diligently to remember the actives and your conversations with them. When you see the actives you've already met, they will be impressed that you remembered them. You'll also meet more of the actives. You'll be entertained by a more meaningful skit that symbolizes what their sorority means to them. This third round is getting personal, so if you have questions about the sororities' principles or standards, now is the time to ask.

After Round Three the actives' "hash sessions" are long and tedious. They now have to decide if they really want you as a sister. Truth is, there are often actives that barely know you who got a good feeling about you and will fight for you. If you rubbed someone wrong, there's a chance they'll voice their opinion loudly. These sessions go into the wee hours of the morning. The actives are very aware that if they invite you back to preference night, they are committing to having you as a sister.

Keep in mind these key things:

☞ They want you! Think of the pledging process as if you were interviewing an extended family. Know what you want and expect in your extended family and be prepared to look for it and get it.

☞ It is a compliment when they know all about your hobbies and interests. You're important to them and the best way for the actives to show this is to know about you.

☞ Ask specific questions. By the end of Round Three you must choose three different houses for preference night. Any of these three houses could be your home for the next four years. From day

one of Rush onward, ask questions and get to know the houses, just like they're getting to know you!

Chances are, the active speaking with you is just as nervous as you are. At least a third of them are on the sorority side for the first time. They are under a lot of pressure to make a good impression on you. They want to get the best pledge class for their sorority.

After Round Three, you should have a good feeling, a gut instinct if you will, as to whether or not you could call these women your sisters. Also, now is the time to make double-dog sure you can afford the financial obligations, that you are ready for the emotional and mental commitment, and that you will be able to contribute to and benefit from becoming a member of this group.

Take some time to think about your needs and desires and devise your own questions so you will not only be prepared but also original. Remember, ask open-ended questions—everyone loves to talk about themselves and they appreciate people who are interested enough to ask.

SISTER TALK

As newlyweds, my parents moved to a city where they knew no one. Reading the newspaper one morning while nearly dying of loneliness, my mother saw a notice that the Delta Gamma alumnae group was meeting that night. My mother called the hostess and asked if she could attend. These women welcomed her with open arms and have remained her closest friends to this day. Sororities are not just for college years. Instead, the bonds of friendship are available to members in cities all over the world, for as long as you choose to embrace them.

My mother's sorority friends were very much a part of my youth. I observed the depth of friendship shared by these ladies, a loyalty that few experience in life. I knew that when I went away to college, I too wanted this experience that had been so meaningful in my mother's life.

As a college freshman, I pledged Delta Gamma. We were a diverse group of young ladies in many ways, but we shared the bond of sisterhood. We provided a sense of family while away from our childhood homes. We struggled through hard times, enjoyed each other's joys, and helped each other through those years of discovering who we were.

Today we share in the struggles and triumphs of careers and raising families. Many of my closest friends today are my sorority sisters from my college days. If I ever have a daughter, I hope she will share this wonderful college experience that my mother and I both treasure.

Tiffany Villager
B.A., J.D., director of research, nonprofit media organization

CHAPTER 9 CHECKLIST

- ☑ *Get to know the other women in your Rush group.*
- ☑ *Relax. Relax. Relax.*
- ☑ *Be yourself.*
- ☑ *Remember names and interests of as many actives as possible.*
- ☑ *Be gracious at each house, even if you don't think you're interested.*
- ☑ *Practice sample Rush questions.*
- ☑ *Don't get too upset if one of the houses you liked cuts you.*
- ☑ *Make your decisions thoughtfully.*

NOTES

CHAPTER 10

Let the Good Times Roll

Preference Night is the most magical time of Rush. You've gone through several days of parties and met hundreds of young women. You've selected a few special houses and most probably, any of them would be fine choices for you. Yet through both of our experiences, that one special house shone through like a beacon on Pref Night.

Preference Night is a formal evening. Many sororities may ask the rushees to wear a white dress for this occasion, so you may want to have one ready. The

Members of college fraternities and sororities are more likely to volunteer and be active in civic affairs during adulthood, according to a nationwide study of college graduates. In addition, the survey revealed: Greek-affiliated students are more likely to be involved with college organizations than nonGreek students; Greek-affiliated alumni are more satisfied with their social development during college than nonGreeks; and Greek-affiliated men and women are more likely than nonmembers to contribute financially to charitable and nonprofit organizations and religious groups.

(The survey, conducted by the Center for Advanced Social Research, University of Missouri, used a nationwide sample of 2,200 college and university graduates. The National Interfraternity Conference and the National Panhellenic Conference jointly commissioned the survey.)

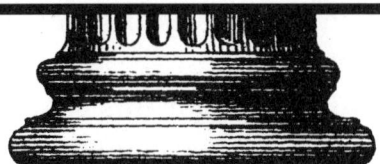

actives will be dressed beautifully. Now's the time to pull out your grandmother's pearls and allow the actives to Rush you! You'll spend about an hour at each house. It is no coincidence that the actives you've met through Rush will greet you at the door and more than likely take you into the living room. You will gather around the fireplace for a fireside chat. These are the girls who have fought for you this far. They are the girls who have made sure you did not get overlooked in the sea of rushees. They want you to be their sister. You could be surprised to see an older sister or aunt who is an alumna that has been brought in to "Rush" you. It could be your childhood friend who pledged the year before you or it could be a new acquaintance that you met during Round Two. Regardless of how long you have known these women, they have helped get you this far.

During this party, expect the actives to lay it on thick. This evening gets very emotional, and there will likely be some tears. There are often candle lighting ceremonies in which the actives will tell you just how special their sorority is to them and how special it will be to you if you pledge their house. They want you to feel as strongly about them as they do about you. One sorority even has petite cakes with each rushee's name written on them. This is to make the rushees feel that they already belong to that house.

After these heart-to-heart chats, the president of the house, the house chaplain, and a few choice actives will give their own testimony of how memorable their college years have become because of the tender moments shared within the walls of their special home. Expect tears and emotions to take over. It's a wonderful evening and afterwards when you sign your card and decide which house best suits you, the experiences had within each house will help clarify your decision. We recommend that you tell the active that you are closest to, in your favorite sorority, how much you like it there and that you plan to put them on the top of your list. This will let her know that you are very serious and hopefully she will make sure you are at the top of their list.

If your heart is set on one sorority and only one, you can "suicide." This is when you put only one choice on your preference card. This is very risky, because you could end up with no bid at all. It is definitely the all-or-nothing choice. Suicide only if you are absolutely sure you would not be happy in any other sorority but your first choice. If you do plan to "suicide," be sure the active you are closest to in that sorority knows your plans. This won't guarantee that you will get their bid, but it will let hem know that your heart is set on them. We don't recommend this approach. Usually one special sorority will shine through, but thousands of rushees have ended up pledging their second or third choices without regret. We recommend that you trust your instincts. When you ask women how they recognized the man they were supposed to marry, the answer is usually, "I just knew." Which sorority is right for you? Trust us, after you have gone through this process, you will "just know!"

Signing on the Dotted Line

After attending all of your Preference Night parties, you will go to the designated place to sign your preference card. This is where you list your sorority choices in your preferential order. It is important to know that you could possibly end up with any of the choices on the card. Just like you filled out your preference card with your choices in order, each sorority submits its preference list with all of the rushees who visited their house on preference night in numerical order beginning with the ones they want the most. Your preference night card is then matched with the sororities' preference lists by a computer. Each sorority has a predetermined quota that they strive to reach. The computer matches rushees to sororities by the sororities' lists and the rushees' preferences. For example, there are 150 girls attending a sorority's preference party. Their quota is 60 bids. Tonya selects ABC sorority as her first choice, DEF sorority as her second, and XYZ as her third choice. Several different matches could occur, according to where Tonya's name appears on each sorority's list.

EXAMPLE 1: Tonya's name is in the top 60 of ABC sorority's list. Tonya will receive a bid from ABC.

EXAMPLE 2: Tonya's name is on the bottom half of the ABC list but on top of DEF's list. Tonya will receive a bid from ABC if enough of the rushees whose names are above hers selected other sororities as their first choice, thus moving her name up the list into the

"My worst Rush memory is one involving one of the first parties, called a Coke party, because—you guessed it—the actives served you Coca-Cola to drink, in those old-fashioned, green glass bottles. After I left a certain house, I heard a rumor that if you didn't ask for a straw to drink your Coke with, you would be cut! Wasn't it enough that I had held my pinky out, like a proper lady?! I was crushed, because this occurred at the house I wanted. After frantically comparing notes with friends—'Did you or didn't you?'—I'm happy to say the rumor was false, because I did get that bid!"

**AMY LYLES WILSON,
B.A., M.A., WRITER**

top 60, or she will receive a bid for DEF because ABC has already filled its quota and her second choice is a match.

EXAMPLE 3: On ABC's list, Tonya's name is #150. On DEF's list, Tonya is #149. XYZ has Tonya listed as #40. It is likely that Tonya will receive a bid from XYZ, her third choice.

EXAMPLE 4: Tonya is on the bottom of all three of her sororities' lists. It is possible that she will not receive a bid. This is a heartbreaking situation, but unfortunately, it does happen. If this does happen to you, try to remember that it is not the end of the world. You can participate in next year's Rush, or carve out a great college life by being involved in many college activities that do not revolve around the Greek system, of which there will be many. We both know of many women who did not get a bid the first time around who later came through Rush and got just what they wanted.

Bid Day

The day after Preference Night, you will be notified if you received a bid. At a designated time, you will go with all the girls in your Rush group who are receiving bids to a specific place. At this time, you will be given an envelope. Inside this envelope lies the name of your sorority affiliation. It could be either your first, second, or third choice. It depends on where you were on the lists. These lists and your "pref" cards are kept top secret. No one will know if you get your first or last choice. Remember, you will be a part of this sorority forever and it is a great honor to be asked to join any sorority. If you did not get your first choice, do not be down and out. No matter which sorority you pledge, you are about to meet a circle of friends that will last a lifetime. If you set your mind to it, you will be happy with the sorority that has chosen you. But if you do get your first choice, congratulations!

Once you accept a bid, you're then on your sorority's list of pledges. You will be whisked away to the house to meet your pledge class and your new sisters, where you'll be welcomed home like a family member. The pledge class will be together for four years and members of the pledge class will become some of your best friends.

The Pledge Period

When you meet your pledge class, you may recognize some girls from your Rush group or other girls you may have met during the week. Keep in mind, some of these girls may become just friendly faces on a huge campus, while others are sure to end up being lifelong confidantes. You will have to find your own place within this group. Your pledge class will elect officers and delegate different responsibilities for the pledge period. Try to get as involved as possible with these activities. The more you put in, the more you will gain.

The pledge period will last from a few weeks to an entire semester, depending on your sorority. During this time, you will be allowed to wear a pledge pin, showing that you are pledging your house. Most sororities don't allow pledges to wear their Greek letters during the pledge period, so they give pledges t-shirts with the sorority's name spelled out and usually designating that they are pledging. There will be special events during the pledge period at which you will be required to wear your pin and t-shirt. The t-shirt will also help you identify your new sisters on campus.

During this time, you will have pledge responsibilities of weekly pledge meetings, weekly dinners, and required study hours designed to make sure you keep up your grades so that you will meet the grade requirement for initiation. During your meetings, you will learn about your sorority's history and expectations of its sisters. There are financial obligations as well as social standards that must be upheld. There are also many social obligations designed to help you get to know your new sisters. Intramural sports, philanthropic activities, and fraternity mixers will also take up your time. The pledge period will be a busy time of your life, and you must practice time management like a corporate executive. While your social life will be buzzing, you must keep in mind that you are there to study and that must be your top priority. And remember: No grades, no initiation!

Initiation

Initiation is one of the most special times of sorority life. After weeks or months of studying your sorority's history, you are now ready to learn its traditions, symbols, and secrets. The initiation ceremony itself is unique to each sorority and highly secretive. You will finally learn the secret handshake, password, and spiritual meanings of your sorority's coat of arms and other symbols. Only sisters of your sorority know this confidential information, and you must promise never to reveal it to anyone.

After the ceremony, you are no longer a pledge but a sister. You will be allowed to wear your Greek letters and your sorority pin. You will be a member of this special group of women forever. You will be responsible for upholding your sorority's good reputation on campus. And just think, next year, you'll be on the other side of Rush!

You are about to embark on the most exciting four years of your life and you are armed with a hundred or so new friends pulling for you, so make the most of it. These are the memories you will tell your granddaughter about when she is about to go through Rush.

Rush is a magical, wonderful experience. We encourage you to embrace and enjoy it. Be yourself and have fun. Best of luck.

SISTER TALK

I often reflect on my college memories, and realize that the lasting friendships created from membership in a sorority become nearer and dearer to my heart as each year passes. Living in the sorority house with fifty other women prepared me for life in ways that I never expected. It taught me time management (you can still shower and get to class on time), organizational skills (it is possible to be a sorority officer, student, and athlete simultaneously), self-discipline (studying for a test instead of going out), and most importantly, how to get along with many different personalities. All of these skills have allowed me to excel in life personally, professionally, and socially.

Honey Hetzel
B.A., career woman and philanthropist

CHAPTER 10 CHECKLIST

- ☑ *Get to know the other women in your Rush group.*
- ☑ *Consider carefully your house choices for Pref Night.*
- ☑ *Dress your best for the Pref parties!*
- ☑ *Don't "go suicide" when choosing a sorority.*
- ☑ *Take the pledging process seriously, and get as involved as possible.*
- ☑ *Be respectful of the initiation ceremony.*

NOTES

Appendix

NATIONAL PANHELLENIC MEMBERS

This is a list of National Panhellenic members. Each national sorority has a governing body, traditions and insignias, publications, funds and philanthropies, and a national headquarters. From chapter to chapter the actives will vary, yet each chapter is governed by its national headquarters. Your campus may have only a few of these sororities or it may have all of them. Your task is to select the best fit for you from among the sororities on your campus.

Alpha Chi Omega
Nickname: Alpha Chi
Founded: DePauw University, 1885
Flower: Red Carnation
Colors: Scarlet and Olive Green
Mascot: Butterfly
Symbol: Lyre

Alpha Delta Pi
Nickname: A D Pi
Founded: Wesleyan College, 1851
Flower: Woodland Violet
Colors: Azure Blue and White
Mascot: Lion
Symbol: Black diamond

Alpha Epsilon Phi
Nickname: A E Phi
Founded: Barnard College, 1909
Flower: Lily of the Valley
Colors: Green and White
Mascot: Giraffe

Alpha Gamma Delta
Nickname: Alpha Gam
Founded: Syracuse University, 1904
Flower: Red and Buff Roses
Colors: Red, Buff, and Green
Mascot: Squirrel
Symbol: Fourteen Pearls

Alpha Omicron Pi
Nickname: A O Pi
Founded: Barnard College of Columbia University, 1897
Flower: Jacqueminot Rose
Color: Cardinal
Mascot: Panda Bear
Symbol: Ruby

Alpha Phi
Founded: Syracuse University, 1872
Flower: Forget Me Not and Lily of the Valley
Colors: Bordeaux and Silver Gray

Alpha Sigma Alpha
Founded: State Normal School, 1901
Flower: Fall flower is Aster; Spring flower is Narcissus
Colors: Crimson Red and Pearl White
Jewels: Pearl and Ruby

Alpha Sigma Tau
Nickname: A S T
Founded: Michigan State Normal College, 1899
Flower: Yellow Rose
Colors: Emerald and Gold
Mascot: Anchor
Jewel: Pearl

Alpha Xi Delta
Nickname: A Xi D
Founded: Lombard College, 1893
Flower: Pink Rose
Colors: Light and Dark Blue and Gold

Chi Omega
Nickname: Chi O
Founded: University of Arkansas, 1895
Flower: White Carnation
Colors: Cardinal and Straw
Mascot: Owl

Delta Delta Delta
Nickname: Tri Delt, Tri Delta
Founded: Boston University, 1888
Flower: Pansy
Colors: Silver, Gold, and Cerulean Blue
Mascot: Dolphin
Symbol: Pearls, Star, and Crescent

Delta Gamma
Nickname: D G
Founded: Lewis School for Girls, 1873
Flower: Cream Rose
Colors: Bronze, Pink, and Blue
Mascot: "Hannah," Raggedy Ann Doll
Symbol: Anchor

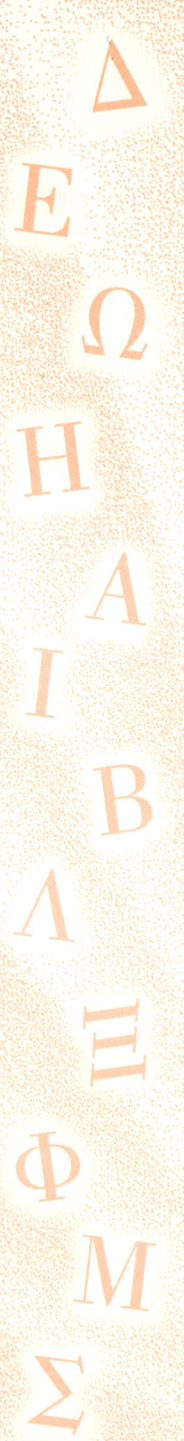

Delta Phi Epsilon
Nickname: D Phi E
Founded: New York University Law School, 1917
Flower: Purple Iris
Colors: Royal Purple and Gold
Mascot: Unicorn
Symbol: Triangle

Delta Zeta
Nickname: D Z
Founded: Miami University, 1902
Flower: Kilarney Rose
Colors: Old Rose and Green
Mascot: Turtle
Symbol: Roman Lamp

Gamma Phi Beta
Nickname: Gamma Phi
Founded: Syracuse University, 1874
Flower: Pink Carnation
Colors: Light and Dark Brown
Mascot: White Harp Seal
Symbol: Crescent Moon

Kappa Alpha Theta
Nickname: Theta
Founded: DePauw University, 1870
Flower: Pansy
Colors: Black and Gold
Mascot: Cat
Symbol: Kite-shaped Badge

Kappa Delta
Nickname: K D
Founded: Longwood College, 1897
Flower: White Rose
Colors: Olive Green and Pearl White
Mascot: Teddy Bear
Symbol: Nautilus Shell

Kappa Kappa Gamma
Nickname: Kappa
Founded: Monmouth College, 1870
Flower: Fleur-de-lis
Colors: Light and Dark Blue
Mascot: Owl
Symbol: Key

Phi Mu
Founded: Wesleyan College, 1852
Flower: Rose Carnation
Colors: Rose and White
Mascot: Ladybug
Symbol: Lion

Phi Sigma Sigma
Founded: Hunter College, 1911
Flower: American Beauty Rose
Colors: King Blue and Gold

Pi Beta Phi
Nickname: Pi Phi
Founded: Monmouth College, 1867
Flower: White Carnation
Colors: Wine and Silver Blue
Mascot: Angel
Symbol: Arrow

Sigma Delta Tau
Nickname: S D T
Founded: Cornell University, 1917
Flower: Golden Tea Rose
Colors: Café au lait and Old Blue
Mascot: Teddy Bear
Symbol: Torch

Sigma Kappa
Nickname: Sigma K
Founded: Colby College, 1874
Flower: Violet
Colors: Lavender and Maroon
Mascot: Snake
Symbol: Dove and Pearl

Sigma Sigma Sigma
Founded: Longview College, 1987
Flower: Purple Violet
Colors: Royal Purple and White
Jewel: Pearl

Theta Phi Alpha
Founded: University of Michigan, 1912
Flower: White Rose
Colors: Silver, Gold, and Blue
Jewel: Sapphire

Zeta Tau Alpha
Nickname: Zeta
Founded: Longwood College, 1898
Flower: White Violet
Colors: Steel Gray and Turquoise Blue
Mascot: Strawberry
Symbol: Crown

OTHER NATIONAL SORORITIES INCLUDE:

Alpha Kappa Alpha
Founded: Howard University, 1908
Flower: Tea Rose
Colors: Apple Green and Salmon Pink
Mascot: Ivy

Delta Sigma Theta
Founded: Howard University, 1913
Flower: African Violet
Colors: Crimson and Cream

Sigma Gamma Rho
Founded: Indianapolis, Indiana, 1922
Flower: Tea Rose
Colors: Royal Blue and Gold

Zeta Phi Beta
Founded: Howard University, 1920
Flower: White Rose
Colors: Royal Blue and Pure White
Mascot: Dove

NOTES

NOTES

NOTES

NOTES